MW00879019

ketogenic diet
DESSERTS
& SWEET SNACKS

DECADENT, GUILT FREE **LOW CARB** *HIGH FAT* DESSERT AND SWEET SNACK RECIPES

Published by The Fruitful Mind

www.fruitfulbooks.com

Disclaimer

TABLE OF CONTENTS

Introduction

If you have never heard of the Ketogenic Diet you don't know what you are missing. Not only does the diet work to help you lose weight but following the diet has many medical benefits. Studies have shown that it works to help control sugar and insulin levels in individuals with diabetes. In addition, the diet also works to help eliminate seizures for people with epilepsy. Some studies have shown that it may even help with Alzheimer's.

A Ketogenic diet replaces carbs with healthy fats. Your meal plan includes recipes that are low carb, medium protein and are high in healthy fats. Eating foods low in carbs and high in fat puts your body into ketosis. Your body is better able to burn fat for energy. Not only will you lose weight, but you will have more energy to get through your day.

One of the biggest reasons that people fall off a diet is those pesky sugar cravings. But on the Ketogenic Diet you can have your cake and eat it too. As long as the cake is low in carbs and high in fat. The recipes in this book all follow the Ketogenic diet guidelines. All of the recipes are made with whole foods. By using these recipes you can satisfy that sweet craving without feeling guilty.

The book is separated into two sections: desserts and sweet snacks. Under desserts you will find yummy treats like Coconut Cream Cake and Raspberry Walnut Parfaits. The snack section includes a collection of recipes for fat bombs, like Almond Joy Bars and Hazelnut Cheesecake Bites. Fat bombs are the perfect way to make sure you eat the required amount of fat for the day.

Fat bombs are small, sweet snacks, made with three basic ingredients. You need a healthy fat, a flavor and a mix in. A serving size for fat bombs is generally one to two pieces. They are the perfect afternoon pick-me-up to give you energy to complete your day. Since the base ingredient for fat bombs is fat, they need to be stored in the freezer or refrigerator to keep them from melting. Enjoy!

ketogenic diet Desserts

BLUEBERRY CHEESECAKE

Who doesn't love a slice of rich, creamy cheesecake? Now you can make a healthy version that won't ruin your diet.

Time to prepare: 20 minutes

Ingredients:

To make the crust:

1 cup raw almonds, unsalted

1 cup shredded coconut, unsweetened

1/4 cup butter, room temperature

1/4 tsp salt

To make the filling:

2 cups cream cheese, room temperature

1 cup heavy cream

1 cup blueberries, fresh or frozen

1 cup granulated sweetener

2 tablespoons lemon juice

1 envelope plain gelatin

2 tablespoons water

To make the topping:

1 cup heavy cream

¼ cup granulated sweetener

1/4 cup reserved blueberry mixture

Directions:

Lightly grease a 9-inch pie plate.

For the crust: Place the almonds, coconut, butter and salt in a blender or food processor. Process till ingredients are thoroughly combined. Pour the mixture into the pie plate and press firmly along the bottom and up the sides.

For the filling: Add the water to a small sauce pot. Sprinkle in the gelatin and bring to a boil. Stir constantly till all of the gelatin is dissolved. Remove from heat and let cool.

Combine the berries and lemon juice in a blender or food processor and pulse till coarsely chopped.

In a large mixing bowl, add ¾ cup of the berries, cream cheese and sweetener. Beat on high speed till the mixture is smooth. Pour in 1 cup of the cream and continue beating another 2-3 minutes or till mixture begins to thicken.

Add the gelatin in a slow drizzle, beating while you add it. Beat another 2 minutes. Add the filling to the crust.

For the topping: In a medium mixing bowl add the remaining berries, 1 cup cream and sweetener. Beat on high speed till mixture resembles whipped cream. Spread the topping over the filling.

Lightly cover the pie and refrigerate for at least 2 hours or overnight. Slice and serve.

Serves 12

Nutritional information: Serving size 1 slice

360 Calories; 34g Fat; 8g Carbs; 3g Protein

BLUEBERRY LEMON COFFEE CUP CAKES

Yummy lemon cakes with wild blueberries. These cakes are baked in a coffee cup so are fun to serve or give as gifts. Besides being low carb they are nut and gluten free too.

Time to prepare: 10 minutes

Ingredients:

1/2 cup wild blueberries, fresh or frozen

1/2 cup plus 1 teaspoon coconut flour

1/4 cup natural sweetener or sugar substitute

1 teaspoon baking soda

Pinch salt

Zest from one lemon

4 eggs

1/2 cup coconut milk

1/4 cup coconut oil, melted

1/2 teaspoon lemon extract

1/4 teaspoon stevia extract

Directions:

Place the blueberries and 1 teaspoon of the coconut flour in a small mixing bowl. Toss to coat the berries and set aside.

In a large mixing bowl, add the remaining coconut flour, sweetener, baking soda, salt and lemon zest. Stir to combine all the ingredients together.

Add the coconut milk, oil and extracts to the dry ingredients and mix well. Gently fold the blueberries into the batter.

Pour the batter evenly into 5 coffee cups. Microwave each cake separately for about 90 seconds. Check for doneness and cook longer if needed.

Yields 5 cakes

Nutritional information: Serving size is 1 cake
188 Calories; 21g Fat; 10g Carbs; 7g Protein

CAPPUCCINO WHIP

When you find yourself wanting something a little decadent after dinner, try this quick and easy dessert. The mousse is light and airy, so it satisfies your sweet craving without leaving you feeling uncomfortable from overeating.

Time to prepare: 15 minutes

Ingredients:

2 cups cream cheese, room temperature

1 cup heavy cream

½ cup almond milk, unsweetened

1/4 cup strong brewed coffee, completely cooled

1-2 teaspoons coffee extract

1 teaspoon vanilla liquid sweetener

Whole coffee beans for garnish

Directions:

In a large mixing bowl, beat cream cheese and coffee on high speed till smooth. Make sure to scrape down sides of bowl occasionally.

Add the milk, 1 teaspoon coffee extract and the sweetener. Beat till all ingredients are thoroughly combined and smooth. Taste and add more coffee extract or sweetener till it tastes the way you want it to.

Pour in the cream and continue beating till mixture thickens and takes on the texture of a mousse. Spoon into serving dishes or ramekins. Refrigerate at least 30 minutes to an hour before serving. Garnish with coffee beans.

Serves 8

Nutritional information: Serving size ½ cup

284 Calories; 30g Fat; 4g Carbs; 0g Protein

CARAMEL PECAN PIE

A guilt free dessert perfect for the holidays. Gluten free and low carb too. The delicious tastes of salted caramel combined with pecan pie all served up in a healthy shortbread crust.

Time to prepare: 40 minutes

Ingredients:

To make the crust:

2 cups almond flour

1/3 cup butter, melted

2 tablespoons granulated sweetener

1 teaspoon pure vanilla

To make the filling:

1 cup pecans, chopped

3/4 cup almond milk, unsweetened

1/2 cup granulated sweetener

1 tablespoon butter

1 teaspoon Arrowroot powder

3/4 tsp sea salt

1/2 teaspoon pure vanilla

½ teaspoon maple syrup, sugar free

Directions:

Heat the oven to 350 degrees. Lightly grease a 9-inch pie plate.

For the crust: In a medium bowl, combine the flour, butter, sweetener and vanilla. Stir to combine all the ingredients thoroughly. Press on the bottom and sides of the prepared pan. Bake 12-15 minutes or edges have begun to brown. Remove from oven and set aside.

For the filling: In a small sauce pot, combine almond milk, sweetener, butter, arrowroot powder, salt, vanilla and syrup. Cook over medium heat till mixture begins to boil, stirring constantly.

Continue cooking till mixture begins to thicken and turns a nice gold color, about 2-3 minutes. Remove from heat and let cool. Stir in ½ cup of the pecans.

Pour the filling into the crust. Top with the remaining ½ cup pecans. Bake till filling begins to bubble, about 15 minutes. Remove from oven and let cool completely before serving.

Serves 8
Nutritional information: Serving size 1 slice
364 Calories; 36g Fat; 8g Carbs; 8g Protein

CARROT CUPCAKES

This is a smaller version of the ever popular carrot cake. These delicious little cakes are a great way to get the kids to eat more vegetables.

Time to prepare: 50 minutes

Ingredients:

To make the cake:

2 cups carrots, grated

2 eggs

1/2 cup coconut oil

1/4 cup coconut flour

1/4 cup granulated sweetener

1 teaspoon vanilla

1 teaspoon baking powder

1 teaspoon cinnamon

To make the frosting:

1 cup cream cheese, room temperature

¼ cup organic honey

1-2 teaspoons milk

1 teaspoon vanilla

Directions:

For the cake: Heat oven to 350 degrees. Lightly oil a muffin pan, or use paper liners.

In a large mixing bowl combine the coconut flour, baking powder and cinnamon.

Place the carrots, eggs, oil, sweetener and vanilla in a blender or food processor. Process till ingredients are combined but some carrot chunks remain. Pour into the bowl with the dry ingredients. Stir till all ingredients are thoroughly combined.

Pour batter evenly into the prepared muffin pan, filling about 2/3 full. Bake 30-35 minutes or the cupcakes pass the toothpick test. Remove from oven and let cool before frosting.

For the frosting: In a medium mixing bowl add cream cheese, honey and vanilla. Beat on high speed till smooth. Add in milk, one teaspoon at a time, and beat well after each addition. Add more milk if needed till frosting is creamy enough to spread. Spread about 2 tablespoons on each cupcake. Refrigerate till ready to serve.

Yields 12 cupcakes

Nutritional information: Serving size 1 cupcake
207 Calories; 18g Fat; 6g Carbs; 1g Protein

CHOCOLATE UPON CHOCOLATE BUNDT CAKE

This recipe is sure to please any chocolate lover. Rich chocolate cake topped with a smooth, white chocolate glaze. It's like sin on a plate.

Time to prepare: 75 minutes

Ingredients:

To make the cake:

2 cups almond flour

1 cup granulated sweetener

1 cup water

1 cup butter

½ cup cocoa powder, unsweetened

½ cup sour cream

3 eggs

2 tablespoons coconut flour

2 teaspoons vanilla

1 1/2 teaspoons baking soda

1/2 teaspoon salt

To make the glaze:

¼ cup cocoa butter wafers

3 tablespoons powdered sweetener

2 tablespoons heavy cream

1 teaspoon vanilla

Directions:

For the cake: Heat oven to 350 degrees. Lightly grease a Bundt cake pan. In a large mixing bowl, add the almond and coconut flour, sweetener, baking soda and salt. Whisk ingredients together till combined.

In a small saucepan, add butter, cocoa powder and water. Heat over medium heat, stirring constantly till butter melts and ingredients are thoroughly combined. Remove from heat.

Add half the chocolate mix to the dry ingredients and stir will. Once combined, add the remaining chocolate and stir to combine ingredients thoroughly.

Add the eggs, one at a time, stirring after each addition. Stir in the sour cream and vanilla. Pour the cake batter into the prepared pan. Bake 40 – 50 minutes or till the cake passes the toothpick test. Remove from oven and cool completely.

For the glaze: Place the cocoa butter wafers in a small saucepan. Heat over medium heat, stirring constantly, till all the wafers have melted and the mixture is smooth.

Add the powdered sweetener and stir well. Stir in the cream till combined and refrigerate. Stir the glaze about every 5 minutes.

When the glaze has thickened and is white in color, transfer it to a blender. Pulse till the glaze is smooth. If the chocolate hardens too much you can put it in the microwave for about 10 seconds.

When the cake has cooled, use a spoon to pour the glaze over the top, letting it drip down the sides. Once the glaze has hardened, slice and serve.

Yields 8 servings

Nutritional information: Serving size 1 slice

480 Calories; 45g Fat; 15g Carbs; 10g Protein

COCONUT CREAM CAKE

This cake is a coconut lover's dream dessert. Moist layers of cake filled with a coconut cream and covered in coconut frosting. Besides the delicious taste the best part is no carbs and gluten free.

Time to prepare: 25 minutes

Ingredients:

To make the cake:

½ cup cream cheese, softened

3 eggs

2 tablespoons coconut flour

1 tablespoon unsweetened coconut flavored syrup

1 tablespoon coconut cream

To make the filling:

1 cup unsweetened coconut, dried

½ cup coconut cream

3 tablespoons unsweetened coconut flavored syrup

To make the frosting:

1 cup heavy cream

¼ cup coconut cream

1 tablespoon unsweetened coconut flavored syrup

1 teaspoon powdered sweetener

Directions:

For the cake:

Lightly grease an 8x8 inch glass baking dish. Place the cream cheese, eggs, coconut flour, 1 tablespoon syrup and coconut cream into a blender or food processor. Process till the ingredients are smooth, if the batter gets too frothy, let it sit for a minute or two.

Pour half the batter into the prepared baking dish. Microwave for about 3 minutes or till the cake is firm. Let cool and remove from dish. Lightly grease the dish again and cook the second half of the batter. Cut the cakes into 9 equal squares.

For the filling:

In a medium mixing bowl, combine the filling ingredients. Let the mixture sit for about 10 minutes or till all of the liquid is absorbed by the coconut.

For the frosting:

In a medium mixing bowl whip the heavy cream till peaks form. Add the coconut cream, syrup and sweetener. Continue beating until the stiff peaks form and the frosting easily holds its shape.

To serve:

Place one cake square on each dessert plate. Add one tablespoon filling and spread to cover the square. Repeat until each cake is 4 layers. Frost the top and sides and garnish as desired.

Yields 4 cakes

Nutritional information: Serving size 1 cake

543 Calories; 51g Fat; 0g Carbs; 7g Protein

COCONUT CREAM PIE

Two kinds of people exist in this world; those who love coconut and those who can't stand it. If you fall into the first category, you will love this low carb version of the popular dessert.

Time to prepare: 45 minutes

Ingredients:

2 cups raw coconut, grated and divided

2 cans coconut milk, full fat and refrigerated for 24 hours

½ cup gold monk fruit

½ cup macadamia nuts

½ cup powdered sweetener

½ cup raw coconut, grated and toasted

1/4 cup almond flour

2 tablespoons butter, melted

Directions:

Heat oven to 350 degrees.

For the crust: Add the nuts to a blender or food processor and pulse till the nuts are ground very fine. Add almond flour, monk fruit and 1 cup of the grated coconut. Pulse until all the ingredients are ground fine and are the texture of graham cracker crumbs.

Add the melted butter and continue processing till mixture begins to form clumps. Press the mixture on the bottom and sides of a 9 inch pie plate. Bake 10 minutes or till the crust is golden brown. Remove from the oven and let cool.

For the filling: Turn the chilled cans of coconut milk upside down and open, pour off the water and scoop the cream into a large mixing bowl.

Add the sweetener and beat on high speed till stiff peaks begin to form.

Fold in 1 cup of coconut gently. Pour the filling in the crust once it has cooled completely. Chill at least 2 hours before serving. Sprinkle toasted coconut on the top of the pie and serve.

Yields 8 servings

Nutritional information: Serving size 1 slice

530 Calories; 38g Fat; 8g Carbs; 4g Protein

COCONUT RASPBERRY ICE CREAM

A decadent frozen treat that tastes like it came from an ice cream parlor. This recipes can also be used to make delicious homemade popsicles.

Time to prepare: 10 minutes

Ingredients:

1 14-oz can coconut milk, thoroughly chilled

1 ¼ cups raspberries, fresh or frozen

¾ cup water

6 tablespoons powdered sweetener

½ teaspoon coconut extract

Directions:

Open the coconut milk from the bottom and pour off the water. You can save the water to use in another recipe. Place the cream that is left in the can into a medium mixing bowl.

Add 2 tablespoons of the sweetener and the coconut extract. Beat the mixture on high speed till soft peaks form.

Place the raspberries, water and remaining sweetener in a blender or food processor. Process till smooth. Add the raspberry puree to the coconut mixture and stir gently to create a marble effect.

Pour the mixture into a medium sized plastic container that has a tight fitting lid. Freeze about 3 hours or till the mixture is firm.

Serves 8

Nutritional information: Serving size about ¾ cup

89 Calories; 8g Fat; 5g Carbs; 1g Protein

LEMON FAUX DANISH

These lemony treats taste like the Danishes you get from the bakery. Low in carbs and gluten free. Perfect with a cup of coffee for a quick and easy breakfast.

Time to prepare: 35 minutes

Ingredients:

¼ cup cream cheese, room temperature

2 eggs

2 teaspoons sweetener

To make the filling:

1 tablespoon butter, melted

1 tablespoon coconut oil, melted

1 teaspoon sweetener

1 teaspoon lemon zest

Directions:

For the Danish: Beat the cream cheese till smooth in a medium mixing bowl. Add the eggs and sweetener and continue beating till mixture is smooth and creamy.

Divide the mixture evenly between 2 large silicone baking cups. Place the cups on a microwave safe dish and cook in the microwave till done, check for doneness every 20– 30 seconds.

When the Danish is done, use a spoon to make a small "well" in the center. Refrigerate to cool.

For the filling: Pour the melted butter and oil into a small mixing bowl. Stir in the sweetener and lemon zest. Refrigerate till the mixture is cool and no longer clear.

Once the filling has turned yellow, spoon it into the center of the Danishes. Refrigerate until the filling is completely chilled. Remove from the baking cups and serve.

Yields 2 Danishes

Nutritional information: Serving size 1 Danish

383 Calories; 37g Fat; 3g Carbs; 10g Protein

MINI PINA COLADA CHEESECAKES

These little cheesecakes make the perfect summer dessert. Tropical flavors of pineapple and coconut combine in a low carb, gluten free dessert that will be a hit all summer long.

Time to prepare: 30 minutes

Ingredients:

To make the crust:

¾ cups coconut flour

2 eggs, lightly beaten

¼ cup coconut oil, melted

1 tablespoon granulated sweetener

Dash of sea salt

To make the filling:

2 cups cream cheese, room temperature

8 ounce can pineapple chunks, well drained

½ cup granulated sweetener

1 egg, lightly beaten

2 teaspoons vanilla

1/4 cup coconut, grated and unsweetened

Directions:

Heat oven to 350 degrees. Line a muffin pan with paper liners.

For the crust: In a large bowl, mix the flour, eggs, oil, sweetener and salt together till mixture is crumbly and sticks together. Press the crust on the bottoms of the paper liners.

For the filling:

Place the cream cheese, pineapple, sweetener, egg and vanilla into a blender or food processor. Process till ingredients are thoroughly combined and the filling is smooth. Pour over the crusts in the prepared pan.

Sprinkle the tops with the grated coconut. Bake for 20 minutes or till the tops are golden brown. Remove from oven and let cool completely. Once cooled, refrigerate for about one hour before serving.

Yields 12 mini cheesecakes

Nutritional information: Serving size 1 cheesecake

246 Calories; 22g Fat; 10g Carbs; 7g Protein

NO BAKE LEMON TARTS

Zesty, delicious tarts that melt in your mouth. Perfect for a light summer dessert or to take to a party or pot luck. Your guests won't even know they are healthy or sugar free.

Time to prepare: 20 minutes

Ingredients:

To make the crust:

1 cup almond flour

3/4 cup coconut, dried and grated fine

3 tablespoons fresh lemon juice

2 tablespoons granulated sweetener

4 1/2 tablespoons butter, melted

1 1/2 teaspoons vanilla extract

Dash of salt

To make the filling:

½ cup butter, room temperature

1/3 cup fresh lemon juice

1/3 cup almond milk

Grated zest of 2 medium lemons

¼ cup plus 1 tablespoon granulated sweetener

2 teaspoons lemon extract

1 teaspoon vanilla extract

¼ teaspoon salt

Directions:

For the crust: Lightly grease 2 mini-muffin pans. In a medium mixing bowl, combine all of the crust ingredients till thoroughly combined.

Place the dough onto a sheet of waxed paper and form into a log shaped roll. Slice the roll into 24 pieces. Press each slice of dough into the wells of the prepared muffin pan, being sure to cover the bottom and about ½ way up the sides of each well. Refrigerate the crusts till ready to use.

For the filling: In a medium bowl, beat the butter till fluffy. Add in the remaining filling ingredients and continue beating till smooth. Taste and add more sweetener or lemon juice as desired.

Pour the filling into the chilled crusts. Return to the refrigerator and chill until the filling is completely set. Remove the tarts from the pans and serve.

Yields 24 tarts

Nutritional information: Serving size 1 tart

101 Calories; 10g Fat; 2g Carbs; 1g Protein

RASPBERRY WALNUT PARFAITS

Layers of vanilla cream, raspberries and walnuts make up this healthy and delicious parfait. Serve them up in beautiful glasses or mason jars for either a fancy or fun dessert.

Time to prepare: 10 minutes

Ingredients:

½ cup fresh raspberries, rinsed and dried

¼ cup walnuts, coarsely chopped

1 can coconut milk, chilled (not low fat)

10 drops liquid sweetener

1 teaspoon pure vanilla

Directions:

In a medium mixing bowl add the raspberries and nuts. Stir to combine.

In a large mixing bowl, beat the coconut milk, sweetener and vanilla till combined, let sit for about 5 minutes.

Spoon half the vanilla cream evenly into 4 glasses or jars. Top with half the berry mixture.

Repeat the layers ending with the berry, nut mix. Refrigerate till ready to serve.

Serves 4

Nutritional information: Serving size 1 parfait
399 Calories; 37g Fat; 13g Carbs; 8g Protein

SUPER SIMPLE CHOCOLATE ICE CREAM

Who doesn't love chocolate ice cream? Now you can enjoy your favorite frozen treat without any guilt. So delicious even the kids won't know its sugar free.

Total time to prepare: 5 minutes

Ingredients:

1 can coconut milk

2 1/2 tablespoons cocoa powder

1 teaspoon granulated sweetener

Dash of salt

Directions:

Place all ingredients into a blender and process till smooth and combined. Pour the mixture into an ice cream maker and follow the directions. Serve.

Serves 2

Nutritional information: Serving size about ½ cup

318 Calories; 28g Fat; 9g Carbs; 3g Protein

WHIPPED CASHEW MOUSSE

Smooth, creamy and nutty describes this light mousse perfectly. But don't worry, its low carb as well as being gluten free. The perfect ending to a great meal.

Time to prepare: 5 minutes

Ingredients:
½ cup whipping cream

½ cup cream cheese, room temperature

1/3 cup liquid sweetener

2 tablespoons cashew butter, unsweetened

½ teaspoon vanilla

Directions:
Beat the whipping cream at high speed till stiff peaks begin to form.

In a medium mixing bowl, beat cream cheese, sweetener, cashew butter and vanilla till mixture is smooth and creamy.

Add the whip cream and beat on medium speed till the mixture is fluffy and light, about 1-2 minutes. Spoon into 3 dessert glasses and serve immediately.

Serves 3

Nutritional information: Serving size about ¾ cup

340 Calories; 33g Fat; 5g Carbs; 6g Protein

VERY VANILLA ICE CREAM

Smooth, creamy, homemade vanilla ice cream, yummy. This low carb ice cream is perfect on a hot summer day. Add some sugar free root beer and voila, a root beer float that won't ruin your diet.

Time to prepare: 50 minutes

Ingredients:

4 cups heavy cream

1 cup granulated sweetener

2 egg yolks

2 teaspoons pure vanilla

Dash of salt

Directions:

Place the cream, ½ cup of the sweetener and salt into a heavy saucepan. Heat the mixture over medium heat just till it begins to boil, do not let it boil.

Whisk constantly and be sure to scrape the sides and bottom of the pan occasionally. Once bubbles start to form, remove from heat.

In a large mixing bowl, combine the egg yolks and remaining ½ cup sweetener. Pour a small amount of the hot mixture into the egg yolks, stirring constantly. Pour the egg mixture into the pan with the rest of the hot cream mixture.

Cook on low heat, whisking constantly, till mixture begins to thicken, about 10 minutes. Pour into a bowl and cover with plastic making sure the plastic touches the top of the mixture. Refrigerate overnight.

When ready to make the ice cream pour the mixture into your ice cream maker. Follow the manufacturer's directions and churn the ice cream about 20-25 minutes or till it reaches the consistency of soft serve ice cream. Pour into a plastic container with an airtight lid and freeze.

Yields about 10 servings

Nutritional information: Serving size about ¾ cup

420 Calories; 44g Fat; 6g Carbs; 3g Protein

ketogenic
diet

Sweet Snacks

ALMOND BERRY BITES

Creamy, crunchy little bites bursting with blueberries. These delicious treats will satisfy any sweet craving and are good for you too.

Time to prepare: 15 minutes

Ingredients:

1 cup blueberries, fresh or frozen

1 cup butter

¾ cup coconut oil

½ cup cream cheese, room temperature

¼ cup coconut cream

¼ cup almonds, ground fine

2 teaspoons granulated sweetener

Directions:

Line a muffin tin with paper cupcake liners.

Place blueberries, cream cheese and coconut cream into a blender or food processor.

Process till ingredients are thoroughly combined and the mixture is smooth.

Add the butter and coconut oil to a small saucepan and cook over medium low heat till melted. Stir in sweetener and add to the berry mixture.

Process the mixture again until smooth and creamy. Sprinkle 1 teaspoon of the ground almonds on the bottoms of the cupcake liners. Pour the berry mixture evenly over the ground nuts. Freeze for at least one hour before serving.

Yields 12 pieces

Nutritional information: Serving size 1 piece

301 Calories; 33g Fat; 2g Carbs; 1g Protein

ALMOND CHEESECAKE BOMBS

These treats are just the thing when those afternoon snack cravings hit. Low in carbs and just sweet enough to curb that pesky sweet tooth.

Time to prepare: 30 minutes

Ingredients:

½ cup cream cheese, room temperature

½ cup almonds, ground fine

1/4 cup almond butter

2 drops liquid sweetener

Directions:

In a large mixing bowl, add cream cheese, almond butter and sweetener. Beat on high speed till ingredients are combined and the mixture is smooth and creamy. Refrigerate for about 30 minutes.

Using your hands, roll the mixture into about 12 balls. Dip the balls in the ground almonds, rolling them to completely cover all sides. Store in an airtight container in the refrigerator.

Yields 12 pieces

Nutritional information: Serving size 2 pieces

180 Calories; 16g Fat; 4g Carbs; 4g Protein

ALMOND JOY BARS

A healthy version of a popular candy bar that tastes just like the real thing. If you do not like almonds you can leave them out. These tasty bars make a great afternoon snack.

Time to prepare: 45 minutes

Ingredients:

2 cup coconut, unsweetened and finely grated

1/4 cup liquid sweetener

1/3 cup coconut oil, melted

3 squares semisweet chocolate

1 tablespoon coconut oil, not melted

12 whole almonds

Directions:

Place the coconut, melted coconut oil and sweetener in a large mixing bowl. Beat until the mixture forms a soft dough, scraping the sides of the bowl while beating.

Press the mixture evenly on the bottom of a 9x5 inch silicone loaf pan. Freeze till ready to use.

In a small, glass bowl, add the chocolate and 1 tablespoon coconut oil and microwave till melted. Stir and check the mixture every 10 seconds. Pour the chocolate evenly over the coconut layer.

Place the almonds in an evenly spaced row along the top. Put back into the freezer for at least 30 minutes.

Remove from the pan and cut into 12 bars. Store the bars in a plastic zipper bag in the freezer.

Yields 12 bars

Nutritional information: Serving size 1 bar

216 Calories; 22g Fat; 4g Carbs; 2g Protein

BACON MAPLE BITES

These yummy little bites have all the flavor of a bacon maple bar fresh from the bakery. Satisfy two cravings at once, with something sweet and savory at the same time.

Time to prepare: 25 minutes

Ingredients:

1 cup cream cheese, room temperature

8 slices bacon, cooked crisp and crumbled

½ cup butter, room temperature

¼ cup maple syrup, sugar free

4 tablespoons coconut oil

4 teaspoons bacon fat

Directions:

Line a small loaf pan with waxed paper.

Place all ingredients into a small glass bowl, making sure to save some of the crumbled bacon for garnish. Microwave, checking and stirring every 10 seconds till mixture is melted and smooth.

Pour the mixture into the prepared pan and sprinkle with reserved bacon. Place in the freezer till firm, about 15 minutes.

Remove from the freezer and pull the waxed paper out of the pan. Cut once down the middle lengthwise. Then slice each bar into about 9 equal pieces. Store tightly covered in the freezer.

Yields about 18 pieces

Nutritional information: Serving size 2 pieces 258 Calories; 27g Fat; 0g Carbs; 4g Protein

CAFÉ MOCHA BOMB POPS

Creamy little popsicles made from vanilla, chocolate and coffee. It doesn't get any better than this.

Time to prepare: 25 minutes

Ingredients:

¼ cup butter, melted

4 tablespoons coconut oil

2 tablespoons heavy cream

1 ½ tablespoons cocoa powder

¾ teaspoons liquid sweetener

½ teaspoon coffee extract

½ teaspoon vanilla extract

Directions:

Line a mini muffin tin with paper liners.

For the vanilla layer: Pour the melted butter into a small mixing bowl. Add the cream and stir to combine. Set aside to cool. Once cool stir in the vanilla.

Pour the vanilla mixture evenly into the prepared muffin pan. Refrigerate till firm, about 15 minutes.

For the coffee layer: In a small mixing bowl combine the coconut oil, cocoa powder, sweetener and coffee extract. Stir till all ingredients are thoroughly combined.

When the vanilla layer has set, pour the coffee mixture evenly over the vanilla layer. Add popsicle sticks and freeze till firm, about 20 – 30 minutes. Remove paper liners and serve.

Yields about 12 pops

Nutritional information: Serving size 2 pops

167 Calories; 18g Fat; 0g Carbs; 0g Protein

CHOCOLATE COVERED STRAWBERRY BOMBS

Smooth rich chocolate surrounds a creamy strawberry center. These little treats are almost too pretty to eat, but go ahead, they are guilt free.

Time to prepare: 15 minutes

Ingredients:

To make the chocolate:

½ cup granulated sweetener

4 tablespoons coconut oil

4 tablespoons butter, room temperature

2 tablespoons cocoa powder, unsweetened

To make the strawberry:

¼ cup strawberries, rinsed and hulled

2 tablespoons granulated sweetener

1 tablespoon heavy cream

1 tablespoon butter

1 tablespoon coconut oil

Directions:

Line a muffin tin with paper cupcake liners.

For the chocolate: In a small mixing bowl, combine sweetener, coconut oil, butter and cocoa powder. Beat on high speed with a hand mixer till ingredients are thoroughly combined and the mixture is smooth. Pour the chocolate evenly among the cupcake liners.

For the strawberry center: Place the strawberries into a blender or food processor and pulse till the berries are pureed. Pour the berries into a small, glass mixing bowl and add the cream. Stir to combine. Microwave the mixture for 10 seconds, set aside.

In a small saucepan, over medium low heat, melt the butter. Add the butter, coconut oil and sweetener to the warm berry mixture. Whisk rapidly till all ingredients are combined.
Spoon the strawberry mixture in the center of the chocolate.

Use a toothpick to swirl the strawberry into the chocolate creating a marble effect. Freeze for at least one hour before serving.

Yields 12 pieces

Nutritional information: Serving size 1 piece

98 Calories; 11g Fat; 2g Carbs; 0g Protein

CINNAMON BITES

Creamy little treats flavored with cinnamon and nutmeg. If you are not a coconut lover, you could roll the treats in ground nuts of your choice.

Time to prepare: 35 minutes

Ingredients:

1 cup coconut, unsweetened and grated

1 cup coconut milk, unsweetened

1 cup coconut butter

1 teaspoon granulated sweetener

1 teaspoon vanilla

½ teaspoon cinnamon

½ teaspoon nutmeg

Directions:

Place the milk, butter, sweetener, vanilla and spices in the top of a double boiler. Cook over medium heat, stirring often, till butter is melted and the mixture is smooth.

Remove from heat. Pour the mixture into a mixing bowl, cover and refrigerate for at least 20 minutes.

Line a cookie sheet with parchment or wax paper. When the dough has chilled enough to handle, use your hands and form into 1 inch balls. Roll the balls in the grated coconut and place on the paper lined cookie sheet. Freeze at least one hour before serving.

Yields about 20 pieces

Nutritional information: Serving size 2 pieces

273 Calories; 30g Fat; 2g Carbs; 1g Protein

DOUBLE CHOCOLATE BITES

The flavors of two popular treats, chocolate ice cream and chocolate chip cookies, in one tasty little treat.

Time to prepare: 10 minutes

Ingredients:

1 cup cream cheese, room temperature

½ cup butter

½ cup granulated sweetener

1/4 cup water

1/4 cup unsweetened cocoa powder

1/4 cup chocolate chips

Directions:

In a small mixing bowl stir together the cocoa powder and water till the mixture forms a thick paste.

In a large mixing bowl, add the cocoa mixture, butter, cream cheese and sweetener. Beat on high speed till mixture is smooth and creamy, about 2-3 minutes. Fold in the chocolate chips.

Place in the refrigerator for about 30 minutes to an hour to firm up.

Line a cookie sheet with parchment or wax paper. Form the dough into about 16 1-inch balls. Place the balls on the paper lined cookie sheet.

Freeze at least one hour. Store in airtight container in the freezer. Let sit at room temperature about 5-10 minutes before serving.

Yields 16 pieces

Nutritional information: Serving size 2 pieces
260 Calories; 24g Fat; 5g Carbs; 2g Protein

EASY FUDGE

Here is a great recipe for melt in your mouth fudge. Yep, fudge that is allowed on a diet. No sugar and no guilt.

Time to prepare: 35 minutes

Ingredients:

1 ¼ cups coconut oil

1 cup pecans, ground fine

¼ cup butter

¼ cup creamed coconut

6 tablespoons cocoa powder, unsweetened

2 tablespoons honey

1 tablespoon pure vanilla

¼ teaspoon sea salt

Directions:

Line an 8x8 inch glass baking dish with wax paper.

Place the coconut oil and butter in a glass measuring cup. Fill a medium saucepan halfway with water. Bring the water to a boil and place the glass cup in the pan. Simmer, and stir the mixture till completely melted.

Pour into a blender or food processor and add the remaining ingredients except the nuts. Blend till all of the ingredients are thoroughly combined. Add the nuts and blend again till the mixture is smooth.

Pour the mixture into the prepared baking dish. Place in the freezer to cool and the fudge is almost completely set.

Remove from freezer and cut into 32 pieces. Store the fudge in a plastic container with a tight fitting lid in the freezer.

Yields 32 pieces

Nutritional information: Serving size 2 pieces
70 Calories; 7g Fat; 1g Carbs; 0g Protein

EASY PEASY PECAN ORANGE BITES

No mess, no fuss with these tempting little treats. The recipe only makes one serving, but you can easily double or triple it so that you will have more on hand.

Time to prepare: 10 minutes

Ingredients:

4 pecan halves, unsalted

1/8 cup cream cheese, room temperature

½ tablespoon butter, room temperature

½ teaspoon orange zest, finely shredded

Directions:

Heat oven to 350 degrees.

Place the pecans on a small cookie sheet and toast about 8 – 10 minutes. Stirring about halfway through. Remove from oven and let cool completely.

In a small mixing bowl, beat together the cream cheese, butter and zest till smooth.

Spread half the cheese mixture onto one pecan half and top with another pecan. Repeat.
Serve immediately.

Yields 2 pieces

Nutritional information: Serving size 2 pieces

163 Calories; 16g Fat; 1g Carbs; 3g Protein

HAZELNUT LOW CARB CHEESECAKE BITES

Nutty little cheesecake bites that taste divine. If you are not fond of hazelnuts, or they are hard to find, you could substitute any nut in their place.

Total time to prepare: 25 minutes

Ingredients:

1 cup cream cheese, room temperature

1/4 cup cocoa powder

1/4 c hazelnuts, ground fine

 2 tablespoons hazelnut syrup, sugar free

Directions:

Place the cream cheese into a large mixing bowl. Add the cocoa powder and syrup and stir to blend the ingredients together.

Using your hands, roll the mixture into about 16 balls. Roll the balls in the ground nuts to cover them completely.

Place on a waxed paper lined cookie sheet and freeze till firm. Then store them in a zippered plastic bag in the freezer.

Yields 16 bites

Nutritional information: Serving size 2 bites

112 Calories; 10g Fat; 4g Carbs; 3g Protein

KEY LIME CHEESECAKE BOMBS

These lime flavored snacks are perfect in the spring and summer. The taste of fresh lime and cheesecake is sure to put a smile on your face.

Time to prepare: 10 minutes

Ingredients:

½ cup cream cheese, room temperature

¼ cup butter, room temperature

¼ cup coconut oil, melted

1 tablespoon lime zest, finely shredded

2 teaspoons granulated sweetener

1 teaspoon fresh lime juice

Directions:

Line a muffin pan with paper cupcake liners.

In a large mixing bowl, beat cream cheese, butter, oil, zest, sweetener and lime juice together.

Beat on high speed till all ingredients are combined and the mixture is smooth and creamy. Pour evenly into cupcake liners. Freeze overnight before serving.

Yields 12 pieces

Nutritional information: Serving size 1 piece 98 Calories; 11g Fat; 0g Carbs; 1g Protein

NUTTY BERRY BITES

Delicious little snacks full of flavor. These treats combine fresh blackberries with macadamia nuts and a creamy cheesecake type layer.

Time to prepare: 15 minutes

Ingredients:

1 cup blackberries; fresh

1 cup coconut butter

1 cup coconut oil

½ cup cream cheese, room temperature

¼ cup macadamia nuts, ground fine

3 tablespoons mascarpone cheese

½ teaspoon fresh lemon juice

½ teaspoon vanilla

Directions:

Heat oven to 325 degrees.

Press the ground nuts on the bottom of an 8x8 inch baking dish. Bake about 7 minutes or till the crust is golden brown. Remove from oven and let cool.

Place the blackberries in a blender or food processor and pulse till the berries are pureed. Pour the pureed berries into a medium sized mixing bowl.

Add the mascarpone cheese, coconut butter, coconut oil, lemon juice and vanilla to the pureed berries. Beat on medium speed till the ingredients are thoroughly combined and the mixture is smooth.

Spread the cream cheese over the nut crust. Pour the berry mixture evenly over the cream cheese layer. Freeze at least one hour.

Remove from freezer and cut into 1 inch squares. Store in an airtight container in the refrigerator till ready to eat.

Yields about 64 pieces

Nutritional information: Serving size 2 pieces

144 Calories; 16g Fat; 1g Carbs; 1g Protein

PEPPERMINT COCONUT BOMBS

Beautifully layered treats that melt in the mouth. A white layer flavored with cool peppermint topped with a creamy chocolate layer.

Time to prepare: 20 minutes

Ingredients:

To make the peppermint layer:

¾ cup coconut butter

1/3 cup coconut, grated and unsweetened

1 tablespoon coconut oil, melted

½ teaspoon peppermint extract

To make the chocolate layer:

2 tablespoons coconut oil, melted

2 teaspoons cocoa powder

Directions:

Line 2 mini muffin tins with paper cupcake liners. For the peppermint layer: In a small mixing bowl, combine coconut butter, coconut, oil and peppermint extract.

Beat on medium speed till ingredients are thoroughly combined and the mixture is smooth. Pour evenly into prepared mini muffin tins. Refrigerate about 15 minutes or the mixture has hardened.

For the chocolate layer: In a small mixing bowl, combine the coconut oil and cocoa powder, mixing well. Pour evenly over the hardened peppermint layer. Refrigerate till firm. Before serving, let sit on the counter about 5 minutes.

Yields about 24 pieces

Nutritional information: Serving size 2 pieces

155 Calories; 18g Fat; 0g Carbs; 0g Protein

PUMPKIN PECAN FUDGE

All the wonderful tastes of fall come together in these easy to make treats. Pumpkin, pecans and cheesecake, delicious. Tastes like cheesecake with melt-in-your mouth texture of creamy fudge.

Time to prepare: 10 minutes

Ingredients:
½ cup butter

½ cup pumpkin, pureed

1/3 cup cream cheese

¼ cup pecans, chopped

2 tablespoons sweetener

2 teaspoons vanilla

1 teaspoon cinnamon

½ teaspoon pumpkin pie spice

1/8 teaspoon salt

Directions:

Line a 9-inch square pan with wax paper. In a medium saucepan, over medium high heat, add butter and stir till melted.

Add the pumpkin. Whisk the butter and pumpkin together till thoroughly combined.

Add the cream cheese, sweetener, nuts and spices and whisk ingredients together till smooth. Add the vanilla and stir just till combined.

Pour the fudge into the prepared pan. Cover and freeze for 24 hours.

Remove the fudge from the pan and cut into 1-inch squares. Store in an airtight container in the refrigerator or freezer.

Yields about 81 pieces

Nutritional information: Serving size 3 pieces

47 Calories; 5g Fat; 0.5g Carbs; 0.5g Protein

SPICED ALMOND BARS

Creamy almond butter mixed with allspice gives these delicious bites a bit of a kick.

Total time to prepare: 5 minutes

Ingredients:

2 tablespoons almond butter

2 tablespoons almonds, coarsely chopped

1 tablespoon coconut oil

1 tablespoon heavy cream

1 teaspoon cocoa powder

¼ teaspoon allspice

Directions:

Line a small loaf pan with waxed paper, being sure the paper comes at least halfway up the sides.

Place the almond butter into a small mixing bowl. Add the oil, cream, cocoa powder and allspice.

Beat on medium speed till all the ingredients are combined and mixture is smooth.

Press the mixture into the prepared pan. Sprinkle the chopped almonds evenly over the top. Freeze about 2 hours or till completely firm.

Remove the mixture from the pan. Cut once down the middle lengthwise. Then slice each bar into about 9 equal pieces. Store tightly covered in the freezer.

Yields 18 pieces

Nutritional information: Serving size 2 pieces

41 Calories; 4g Fat; 1g Carbs; 1g Protein

CONCLUSION

Let's face it, sticking to any diet is hard work. We all know that dieting is often necessary. Whether you diet to lose weight, or improve your overall health, you will be tempted along the way. Most people fall of the diet wagon because they need to satisfy those pesky sweet cravings. This reason, among others, is why this book is so helpful.

Now you have recipes to help you stay on track. Worried about those holiday dinners? Don't, just prepare one of the tasty desserts to take with you. Feeling run down in the afternoon? Just treat yourself to one of the recipes found in the snack section. All of the bites and bombs are designed to help you meet your fat intake for the day plus give your body the fuel it needs to keep going till dinner time.

Following the Ketogenic diet is much easier than most people realize. Just be sure to pay attention to what you are eating. Make a meal plan in the beginning of the week and be sure to stick with it. And dieting alone will not help you to lose weight. Be sure to include some physical exercise every day. Good luck!

16117109R00051

Printed in Great Britain
by Amazon